DISCOVER!

EARTH AND SPACE SCIENCE

ROCKS AND MINERALS

Beth Irving

Enslow PUBLISHING

Please visit our website, www.enslow.com. For a free color catalog of all our high-quality books, call toll free 1-800-398-2504 or fax 1-877-980-4454.

Cataloging-in-Publication Data
Names: Irving, Beth.
Title: Rocks and minerals / Beth Irving.
Description: Buffalo, NY : Enslow Publishing, 2027. | Series: Earth and space science | Includes glossary and index.
Identifiers: ISBN 9781978550322 (pbk.) | ISBN 9781978550339 (library bound) | ISBN 9781978550346 (ebook)
Subjects: LCSH: Rocks–Juvenile literature. | Minerals–Juvenile literature.
Classification: LCC QE432.2 I785 2027 | DDC 552–dc23

Published in 2027 by
Enslow Publishing
2544 Clinton Street
Buffalo, NY 14224

Designer: Claire Vanden Branden
Editor: Noah Riccardi

Photo Credits: Cover, p. 1 mineral vision/Shutterstock.com; p. 5 M. Chapin/Shutterstock.com; p. 7 Ralf Lehmann/Shutterstock.com; p. 9 Chris Curtis/Shutterstock.com; p. 11 Lodolite Studios/Shutterstock.com; p. 13 Stefan Malloch/Shutterstock.com; p. 15 Cavan-Images/Shutterstock.com; p. 17 Zik G./Shutterstock.com; p. 19 Jonas D. Bell/Shutterstock.com; p. 21 zhukovvvlad/Shutterstock.com.

Printed in China

CPSIA compliance information: Batch #QS27ENS: For further information contact Enslow Publishing, at 1-800-398-2504.

CONTENTS

BOLDFACE WORDS APPEAR IN THE GLOSSARY.

PLANET EARTH

Earth is huge. It's really old, too. Do you know what Earth is made of?

Planet Earth is made up of rocks and minerals. We see rocks and minerals all around us. Rocks make up the ground we walk on. They form the bottom of the ocean.

THREE TYPES OF ROCKS

There are three types of rocks. One type of rock comes from **lava**. Lava is a very hot **liquid**. Earth makes it under the ground.

When lava comes out onto the **surface**, it cools and becomes hard rock. It forms **igneous** rock.

Another type of rock comes from pressing mud and sand together. Over a very long time, it gets harder and becomes a rock. This is called a **sedimentary** rock.

The third type of rock is made by changing rocks after they are made. Sometimes Earth presses so hard on rocks that it changes them. These are called **metamorphic** rocks.

FINDING FOSSILS

Sometimes, the bodies of plants and animals get stuck in rocks! They leave remains called **fossils**. They get stuck in sedimentary rocks while the rocks are forming.

Fossils can help people learn about Earth's history. We know dinosaurs existed because of fossils.

ALL ABOUT MINERALS

Minerals are the building blocks of rock. All rocks are made of minerals. Minerals can change how rocks look.

Each kind of mineral is made of specific **elements**. For example, the common mineral called quartz contains the elements silicon and oxygen.

There are so many different minerals. Some minerals can be really interesting. Diamond is one of the hardest materials in the world. A mineral called talc can break apart in your hands. Pyrite is a mineral that can naturally form perfect cubes. Graphite is a mineral, too. We use it as pencil lead.

The image on page 15 shows a mineral called rhodochrosite. It can form strange and beautiful shapes.

Some minerals help us stay healthy. Milk has a mineral called **calcium**. Calcium gives us strong bones and teeth. We also need iron to live. It's a mineral that makes us stronger. We get iron when we eat vegetables.

Minerals can also help us learn. By studying a mineral called zircon, people found the oldest rocks on earth. They were over 4 billion years old.

FAMILY OWNED
Sunnyside FARMS
HIGHEST QUALITY
FROM LOCAL DAIRIES
WHOLE MILK
VITAMIN D • PASTEURIZED
EXCELLENT SOURCE OF CALCIUM
GRADE A
REAL CALIFORNIA MILK
PERISHABLE
KEEP REFRIGERATED
Nutrition Facts
16 servings per container
Serving size 1 cup (240mL)
Calories per serving 160
Total Fat 8g 10%
Sat. Fat 5g 25%
Trans Fat 0g
Cholesterol 25mg 8%
Sodium 110mg 5%
Total Carb. 12g 4%
Fiber 0g 0%
Total Sugars 12g
Incl. 0g Added Sugars 0%
Protein 8g 16%
WHOLE MILK
Nutrition Facts
16 servings per container
Calories per serving 160

USING ROCKS AND MINERALS

Some scientists study Earth for their jobs. They use rocks and minerals to learn about Earth. This helps us understand where we live.

We learn about Earth in school, too. Sometimes your teacher will bring in rocks and minerals. You get to hold them and look at them.

We use rocks and minerals to build buildings. The rocks make the buildings strong. They keep the buildings safe from bad weather. They also make the buildings pretty.

Sometimes, people climb on rocks. They climb high into the air. It can be hard, but it's good exercise. Some people think this is a lot of fun!

GLOSSARY

calcium: A mineral that makes bones and teeth strong.

elements: The parts that make up minerals and other materials.

fossils: Remains of animals or plants in a rock.

igneous: Rocks that come from lava.

lava: Hot, liquid rock that comes out of Earth.

liquid: Something that flows like water.

metamorphic: Rocks that come from changing other rocks.

sedimentary: Rocks that come from sand or mud that gets harder over time.

surface: The outside layer of something.

FOR MORE INFORMATION

Books

Carlson-Berne, Emma. *Let's Explore the Rock Cycle*. Minneapolis, MN: Lerner Publications, 2021.

Murray, Julie. *Rocks*. Minneapolis, MN: Abdo Publishing, 2025.

Websites

Britannica Kids: Rock
kids.britannica.com/kids/article/rock/404136
Learn more about rocks at this site.

National Geographic Kids: Geology
kids.nationalgeographic.com/science/article/geology-101
Learn about geology, the study of rocks.

Publisher's note to educators and parents: Our editors have carefully reviewed these websites to ensure that they are suitable for students. Many websites change frequently, however, and we cannot guarantee that a site's future contents will continue to meet our high standards of quality and educational value. Be advised that students should be closely supervised whenever they access the internet.

INDEX